Five Sleazy Sli

Phil Berto

Five Sleazy Slippets And A Missive Or Two

Phil Berto's Snippets Series, Volume 7

Phil Berto

Published by Stormy Summers Publishing, 2020.

FIVE SLEAZY SLIPPETS AND A MISSIVE OR TWO

First edition. November 29, 2020.

Written by Phil Berto.

DEDICATION

#######

The very first time we Americans were confronted by a pinch faced bureaucrat peddling politically-correct bullshit, we should have told him/her/undecided to go fuck him/her/itself.

Ditto the LGBT-WTF, BLM and ANTIFA thugs.

This book is for those who do so now.

LIB-RALS UNWITTINGLY SUPPORT RACIST IDENTITY POLITICS AND WANT YOU TO.

Before you let racist BLM Marxists or racist Supremacists color your thinking, consider the simple words of two geniuses.

"We're all in this together." -Judge Mathis

"I didn't pick you either." -Phil Berto

Also by Phil Berto:
SNIPPETS – COMMENTS FROM THE RED
SNIPPED – AMERICA POST #ME TOO
SNIPS – COMMENTS FROM THE BLACK AND BLUE
SNAPPED – COMMENTS FROM A C-C-CONSERVA-
TIVE
SNAPPER – THE LIBERAL FINGER
UNSNAPPED – OBEDIENT LIB-RAL EDITION
FIVE SLEAZY SLIPPETS AND A MISSIVE OR TWO

VISIT WWW.PHILBERTO.COM[1]

---

1. http://WWW.PHILBERTO.COM/

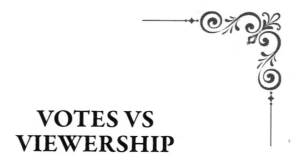

VOTES VS
VIEWERSHIP

Thank you, Fox News, for the tiny story about a van in a parking lot. May we now look forward to something on, say, SMARTMATIC/DOMINION?

SHEEPLE GET THE GOV-MINT THEY DESERVE

Hey Moe! Let's source (yuppie for "get") our vote tabulators from China. It's not like one of the candidates has corrupt ties to Chinese Communists. Oops!

BIG

#######

PENNSYLVANIA

CNN: How many votes did we... Did Biden get to-day?

Gov: How many do we... Does he need?

CNN: Don't lib-rals know they're voting for big pharma, big banks, etc.?

Gov: You and big tech and big teaching won't tell them, so no. No, they don't.

HE DIDN'T RELISH IT

The Pope was in a pickle. To support the most pro-life president the U. S. A. has ever known, he'd have to stop shoving unvetted, unvaccinated, unemployed illegal alien invaders into our Country via Catholic Services and the fugitives they harbor in other people's neighborhoods. If Papa Francisco backed Open Borders Biden, he'd have chosen a Catholic candidate who champions late-term and partial-birth infanticide. The only way out was to go infallible, which he did, the same way all of us go infallible: he shut the fuck up. Thank you Jay-is-us. That was big.

PS: One (1) U. S. Bishop grew a pair and went very public in condemning late-term abortion. (Name withheld to prevent lib-ral listing.)

Catholic Services: gives fugitives OPM, hides them in OPN*

*Other People's Money/Neighborhoods

BLUE STATE

Did Biden win yet? No? Okay, no more signature checks.

Did Biden win yet? No? Okay, no more postmark checks.

Did Biden win yet? No? Okay, accept "ballots" 'til Friday.*

"It takes longer when the election is close." - PA A. G.

Translation: We'll keep counting "ballots" 'til Biden wins.

*Friday starts the weekend, so, let's say Monday, Midnight Monday.

NO VOTER FRAUD

CNN, CBS, NBC, MSNBC, PBS, DNC: There is no voter fraud.

FOX NEWS: If there is no fraud, why won't they let us monitor the count?

CNN, CBS, NBC, NBC, PBS, DNC: Because there is no voter fraud!

JOKE

I never thought Biden was funny until he called for "calm" as if it wasn't his people who had rioted for 6 months.

NO JOKE

California voters (alive and dead) rejected racial preference perks. How racist! The entire State should doxx/list/boycott itself. AOC & friends are en route to re-educate.

JOEKAMMY VOTER

Loves lockdowns; hates National Guard citizen-soldiers protecting lives & property. Joke-a-me.

DON'T MOCK IT 'TILL YOU'VE TRIED IT

Yuppies think my typewriter is quaint. So, I think talking in questions is stupid? They will never know that typing has a feel to it (Yes, I am that needy) as the keys slap the paper. Diddling on a computer keypad must be like taking a riding crop to an inflatable lady: the sound is there but not the effect. Not that I've ever...

Note: The Girl and I bought a short riding crop, which she called a bat, at, of all places, a Western tack & saddle shop. Cashier Lynda Sue turned bright red when I allowed as these things are sometimes used on horses, doncha know?

HARDON A FELLER

Working at CNN has given once-honest Jake a permanent wince.

Q: Why does he remain a corporatist tool?

A: Pay. Can't make that jack teachin' school.

Q: But... But Don seems serene, no?

A: 1-Don don't know he's lying;

2-He finally reaches his desk with his milk money.

HIGH SCHOOL DIPLOMA

Ask any product of NEA (union, no competency testing) teaching what exactly they did for twelve fucking years. Answer:

THE SILENCE OF THE LAMBS

It's been 3 generations since the '60s. The sheeple are ready; the dumbdown is completed. We can now get 51% of the population to toss a populist president (Remember "Power To The People"? Of course you don't. Three tiers of tenured hoaxes have erased that shit.) and support 1/2-century (How 'bout: "Never trust anyone over 30"? They canceled that, too?) career big gov-mint bureaucrat who smarms into power via sleazy side deals with China, Russia & Ukraine (the real collusion), promises to Big Tech, Big Labor, Big Banks, Big pharma, Big Media, Big Teaching, Big Globalists, Big Corporatists, Big P-P-P-Pentagon (Remember the March on the P-P-Pentagon? Librals were less obedient back then.) Now the sheeple will, in effect, weaken their own Country, raise their own taxes, and give up their freedom of speech, which is already half-gone thanks to cowardly political correctness and censorship by Big Tech. All that's left is to get half of them on the dole so they'll have to vote Democrat to "keep our shit coming". This, of course, is Pelosi's wet dream. She does not count sheep. She counts sheeple. Dumbass.

TRUMP DID MORE FOR BLACK FOLKS IN 4 YEARS THAN OBIDEN DID IN 8. DUMBASS.

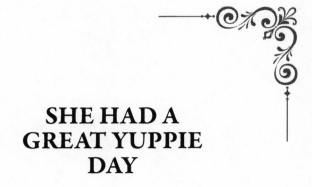

SHE HAD A GREAT YUPPIE DAY

Hugged a tree, bought Bounty and "sea" salt, and ran over 3 snakes. Kumbaya.

ARITHMETIC
REGRESSION

Covid testing doubled; cases didn't.*
Q: When will CNN say the rate is dropping?
A: When Trump isn't President.
*2x tests, 1x more cases

SUPPOSE THEY GAVE A PARIS ACCORD

AND NOBODY CAME?

TECH TIP

This just in: 'Steemed publisher assures me that computer keypads can be induced to make typewriter noises. Yay. But do you see it smack the paper, like a riding crop (there you go again.-Editrix) slapping Rhonda's round...

So, get back to me when you can teach it yuppiespeak?

Yuppiespeak: so, like when Duke Energy uses a second sheet of (3/4 blank) paper to invite me to "go online" (of course) to "consult the tutorial" (swear to God) to "explore the enhancements of my new bill"? (So, you think I'm making this up, don't you?)

Q: So, what do yuppies do after wasting 3/4 of a sheet of paper on bullshit?

A: So, they hug a tree and buy Bounty?

PS: When publishers call you "Fred Flintstone", it's a compliment, right?

THE SHAME OF THE CELERY

When did Americans start hiding their groceries? Buy a sack of potatoes, they put it in a bag. Onions in a bag? Quick, bag 'em up! Six pack of soda, beer, water, whatever with a nice handle onnit? Pshaw! Here's a chance to use up another bag. Just as pharmacists are paid by the staple, I believe grocery cashiers are bonused by the bag. Two things I do want stuffed into a sack, pronto: the box o' pontoons The Girl asked me to get and, of course, my Depends. Hard to flirt with the clerk-ess when... You know...

SCARY SHIT

She routinely takes turtles, which can snap a finger, from the track; but the Jennings GP cornerworker is afraid to enter the Turn 3 shack because it is co-inhabited by a yearling blacksnake. I understand. Why, hardly a day goes by that a person isn't chased down by a 2-foot blacksnake, which invariably trips them up, crawls up their back, and bites them on the earlobe. Heck, if cornered and harassed, any nonpoisonous (translation: beneficial) snake may bite you, and all are capable of... Trust me on this one... of... of breaking the skin! So be careful out there, Missy. Do not get hunted down and nibbled to death.

PS: When the snake gets offended and moves to the Race Control Tower, EMS will be put on standby for mouse attacks at, you guessed it, Turn 3.

NO WORDS

China pays 2%, has 30 years to clean up its filthy production methods.

U. S. A. pays 90%, cripples ("regulates") our already-clean industry right now.

AY-OCH: "This will save 1° F in 100 years!

Conservative: "You gotta be fucking kidding me."

Progressive: "Where do we sign?"

Lib-ral: JoeKammy (Joke-a-me) will get it back!

SO NOT A
TAXPAYER?

Q: So, you have a 10-year loan on your Prius?
A: So, yes, but only 5 years on my designer washer/
dryer ensemble?
Q: So, which payments are higher?
A: So, my studio apartment rent?
Q: So, isn't that Trump's fault?
A: So, we'll do totally better under Biden?

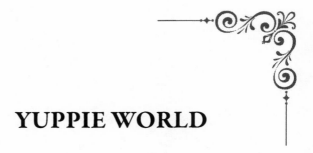

YUPPIE WORLD

#######

S O, ASS BACKWARDS?
My friends in South and Central America* think we
have lost our minds. Having seen the ravages of Socialism first-
hand, they are astounded that we would let big media and big
tech and big pharma and big corporate overthrow (no other
word for it) a populist Washington outsider who was steadily
giving power back to the people and then "elect" a career bureaucrat whose whole family is on the globalist take. (Gee, d'ya
think Pfizer withheld the vaccine 'till the day after the election
by coincidence?) Anyway, once again, the left is accusing the
right of Democrat depredations, and half the population
b'lieves them. Why? Because We The Sheeple has suffered three
generations of ex-hippie parents/friends and NEA (union, no
competency testing) teacher/indoctrinators.

PS: No matter how much of our economic independence
is squandered to world-wide "wealth redistribution" (see: stealing), big corporate's stooges in big media will be fine. Bad news
is big news; their incomes are assured.

*Why not just say "Alabama and Kansas"? -NEA Teacher

SO, YOU CAN'T FIX STUPID?

Just in case a generation of dumbing-down (thank ay teechr) wasn't enough, Big Tech censored conservative thought (but never liberal), Big Pharma ran Scare The Seniors ads, VH-1 and MTV/TEEN MORON MOMS pushed Vote For Your Life lies, (Note: Trayvon Mar-in was <u>not</u> shot for wearing a hoodie), and the Revisionist History Channel aired a documentary about turn of the 20th century robber barons to trick (too easy) today's useful idiots into reinstating a regime that was handpicked by today's robber barons.

Q: So, what's the difference between 19th/20th century robber barons in today's robber barons?

A: So, Big Media, Big Tech, Big pharma, and Big Teacher's Union?

SO, DEMS KNOW THEIR BASE?

Q: So, who has two weeks to vote and still shows up 3 days late?

A: So, people who have 9 months to decide and still get a partial-birth abortion? So, at taxpayer expense?

Q: So, are you saying that deadbeats should not vote?

A: So, or breed? PS: So, for nine months bitch never missed a mani-pedi or a tattoo/piercing appointment? So, also at taxpayer expense?**

**So, you pay for her food so she can buy body bling? So, that means you paid for it? So, you are stupid?

LIKE FATHER, LIKE DOUCHEBAG

Throughout Trump's throes you couldn't wipe the smirk off Chris Wallace's face.

THE "HANDS UP, DON'T SHOOT" LIE BECAME THE "VOTE FOR YOUR LIFE" LIE

The Fox News spin was pathetic. "Trump will have more influence advising* the Party than if he were reelected." Oh, really. Lessee: Second-term Trump would jail Comey, Clapper and Brennan; they couldn't dirty trick the next election. What advice could Trump possibly give Republicans? Don't be hapless? Don't be stupid? Don't be outsmarted by MTV/TEEN MORON MOMS?

What you know:	What MTV allows you to say:
Michael Brown DNA on cop's gun	Michael Brown was shot for jaywalking
Trayvon Martin terrorized neighbors	Trayvon Mar-in shot for wearing hoodie

Q: Who believes this Vote For Your Life bullshit?

A: Bro. They watch Teen Moron Moms. Look for a thought process elsewhere. These NEA projects define "useful idiots".

Teen Moron Mom Mom: "She'll be fine"; her eyes say, "My daughter is stupid".

Teen Moron Mom Dad: "She'll be fine"; his eyes say, "My daughter is a slut".

Yes, she's a stupid slut, but you the taxpayer buy her food stamps so she can spend her welfare check on tattoos and piercings. Compared to you, Mr. & Mrs. taxpayer, that stupid slut is a fucking genius.

Note: In half an hour, Rob Dyrdek will host Parents Pushing Pot.

Question: Is trading food stamps for weed what got your daughter knocked-up?

Teen Moron Mom Mom: Heavens, no! She's not that easy. It took a crack crucial to knock her up. Why d'ya think baby came out kinda twitchy... uh, alert?

Teen Moron Mom Dad: What's a "crucial"?

Teen Moron Mom Mom: uh... Nevermind.

See? Rob Dyrdek is doing illegitimate babies everywhere a favor by pushing pot. Budhead bastards come out nice and mellow. Fer shure.

WARNING: You said "stupid slut". Here come AOC and her lib-ral thought/language po-lice. Quick! Bust a window, boost a Blackberry, and blurt, "Black Lives Matter". CNN will call it a "mostly peaceful protest" and give you a pass for not wearing a mask.

PS: Rob Dyrdek's sidekick, Steelo Brim, sees a ten-year-old white kid on a 20' boat and blurts, "He looks so privileged". Here go more MTV rules.

1-You are the racist, not Steelo Brim.

2-If you are white and on a boat, you are privileged.

3-You are the hater, not Steelo Brim.

*Back to Trump "advising" Gutlessrepublicans: The naïveté is the more astounding coming from usually sharp people. Looking to their own fiefdoms, as always, globalist Gutlessrepublicans will jettison now-"loser" Trump and rush to kiss

Schumer's ass. They will call it "compromise", of course, but Chuck is already washing up.

DEAD DEMS VOTE

Early voting, late voting, dumbed-down voting, pay-for-a-vote voting. None of this was quite gettin' it, so Dems Found A Way to vote after death.

Q: How d'ya stop voting in several states and dead people's votes?

A: Outlaw mail-in ballots except for the military and documented cases.

Q: What about Covid-19?

A: Aw, just stop by and vote on the way to the piercing/tattoo parlor. Dumbass.

ATT OLYMPIC COMMITTEE

Females pour out a bottle and that's that. Males always, like, shake the thing.

A CAUSE WITHOUT A REBEL

"Keep the skeer on 'em, boys!" -Confederate Lt. Gen. Nathan Bedford Forrest

CNN toady Jake Tapper scoured the globe and found a 19 year-old with covid.

"See? See? Covid kills young people, too!" Translation: Hope that Harris/Biden win so you can be obedient to even more grotesque big gov-mint bureaucracy.

BUT "HEIRESS" IS STILL OK

While Robert Redford pecks at a tent peg in Out Of Africa, Meryl Streep's strong fact-based character proudly performs women things and a few man things; her femininity is never in doubt. I remember gals like that.

A: Can a woman kill a charging lion* and remain all-female?

Q: If the woman is Meryl Streep, why, yes. Yes, she can.

*It was a lioness, but if we are not allowed to say, "stewardess"...

MTV

The home of Teen Moron Moms tells you it's cool to vote as you are told. You must shun the anti-establishment outsider who pisses off everyone, including his own Party (always a good sign). MTV wants you to feel hip about supporting a 47-year Old Guard Washington cronie; a card-carrying member of the Party of Lester Maddox & Bull Conner, fire hoses & axe handles, and trade deals that favor China, the Biden family, Big Business, and the Biden family.

Q: How did sheeple get dumbed-down enough to buy into this bullshit?

A: Years of indoctrination by NEA (union, no competency testing) teachers.

Now, go home and do everything that MTV and Teen Mo-ron Moms tell you to do. Be nice, obedient little lib-ral boys & girls, and you'll get a medical brownie.

NEW MATH

Chobani: half as good as store brand + twice the price = four times as dumb.

Hey, at least it doesn't come in cutesy little backwards con-tainers designed just for chicks (hear me roar) that entrap and slowly suffocate baby skunks, squirrels, etc. She'll go, "Aww", every time she sees the footage, but bitch keeps buying the stuff.

Q: Why?

A: Cutesy container. Gotta have it.

Note: No surprise there. These are people who walk around (and drive) with hair covering one eye. see: Teen Mo-ron Moms/Harris-Biden voters. Do~dah.

OBEDIENT GENERATION

The MTV ads are relentless. "Tired? Angry? Depressed? It's been a tough year.

Go to Vote For Your Life.com. we'll tell you what to do." Gee, I wonder which candidate they're harvesting votes for. Someone at Fox News should check out the "nonprofit" donor list. Pro-China/open borders/antifa socialists? 100%.

PS: See? You can vote away "tired". Who knew?

YUPPIE

Hates hunting. Serves lamb and veal that was establishment-killed on a factory farm. Kumbaya.

UNCOOL

In an effort to maintain the status quo (trade deals that favor China,term unlimits, lobby system, grotesque big govmint, etc.), Wall Street money is pouring in to the Biden campaign.

Q: Why do lib-rals think that voting for the establishment is avant garde?

A: Three generations of ex-hippie parent/friends and socialist teachers.

Q: Resulting in...?

A: Useful idiots.

Q: Why don't the Bidens just go home and enjoy their pay-offs?

A: Jail time.

Q: Who calls graft "grift"?

A: Everybody at Fox News.

Q: Whaddya call grifters who take graft?

A: Family Biden.

SEE? SEE? COMPUTERS SAVE PAPER!

The yuppie tree huggers who conjured my new electricity bill Found A Way to complicate the comparison graph and stretch the thing into 1 and 1/4 pages which, of course, requires two (2) sheets of paper which, of course, leaves 1 and 3/

4 pages "intentionally left blank ". The "exciting" new bill invites me to "go online" and "consult a tutorial" (Swear to God) to "explore the enhancements" (You think I am making this up, don't you?}.

If you wonder what kind of mind prefers a corrupt 47-year political hack over a renegade populist who answers only to the people, now you know. Imagine attending a Staff meeting with these goofies.

PS: If I ever "explore the enhancements" of a bill, please shoot me.

FBI OR KGB. (WTF, PICK ONE)

Comey is a big bear of a wus; Putin is a scrappy little shit.

Comey mealy-mouth non-indicted Clinton; Putin was a KGB killer.

Comey is duplicitous; Putin is in-your-face about his position.

Comey tore his Country apart; Putin is a lion in defense of his.

Which would you hire to guard your store, your home, your Country?

IS IT WORTH SAVING?

Its people tamed a wilderness, won two world wars, ended the eons-old institution of slavery in two generations (an eyeblink in human history) and provided a standard of living that is the envy of the world. Now, half the population is on the dole and/or "medical" marijuana, kills its babies up to the moment of birth and calls it a "women's health issue", and has to think about choosing a populist Washington outsider who both Party establishments** fear over a 47-year...I may have already mentioned 47 years of amassing a fortune for doing jack shit other than influence peddling. It kinda begs a bumper sticker: Be Stupid; Vote Joe.

Note: Slavery still exists in Islamic countries, of course. Ilhan. Rashida. Joe.

** If this is not "having the right enemies", what is?

ISLAM SUCKS

Black Muslims reject a religion that once condoned slavery in favor of one that still does.

UNINFORMED BALLOT

Reminiscent of Rock The Vote, MTV/TEEN MORON MOMS and VH-1 now ~~shoehorn~~ crowbar Vote For Your Life detritus (Tired? Depressed? We can fix it by telling you how to vote!) into every crevice of their churlishness. The (Revisionist) History Channel quickly followed suit, dragging out its anti-capitalist docudrama once again, all on the eve of the election. Problem: even with early voting favoring deadbeats who cannot be counted on to present themselves in a timely manner for anything, it's hard to get them to put down the bong long enough to wobble into a polling place.

During a previous election, one of many local dirtbags entered the polls supported by a BLM-type thug on each arm. He was greeted by the Supervisor of Elections, who said, nice as pie, "Oh, Mr. Jones, you already mailed in your ballot". For her trouble, she was given two hateful stares and one addled, "Say, what?". Now, <u>that's</u> what I call an informed ballot.

MORE FINE CUSWEEN

Make that clean cube steak taste like not venison: soak it in milk for twunny minutes, bread and deep fry it. Tell her yuppie friends they are eating Bambi cutlet, but leave out the "Bambi". Thinkin' it was establishment-killed on a factory farm, why, they won't give it a thought. They'll eat lamb and/or veal all day long, s'long as somebody else kills it for them. Can I get a "Kumbaya"?

PS: Special Breakfast from the leftovers: heat, cover with chives, top with a runny egg. Wash it all down with a stout Bloody Mary. Ta-da! Goodbye hangover, hello Sun Salutation*.

*Ast her yoga yuppie friends Whiskey Tango Foxtrot <u>that</u> is.

INNUENDO MEETS INSINUATION

In today's "liberal" world, an accusation often amounts to a conviction.

When Hirono asked Barret if she had ever been accused of a sex crime, I hoped the Judge would counter with, "No, have you?"

Gillibrand Glossary

Lib-ral: views Biden's CBS town hall vs. Trump's NBC Court of Star Chamber and thinks, "Yeah, that's fair".

Note: Trump was questioned by Biden supporters. Biden was questioned by...

Biden supporters.

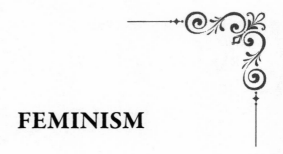

FEMINISM

He called her, "Miss Piggy".
Sexist! Everybody knows it is N. O. W. "Ms. Piggy".

GALA WE PUNISH

OUR ENEMIES SECTION

THE MATH LESSON THAT OBAMA/BIDEN FAILED

"Don't give up the ship!" -John Paul Jones

"The ship to six Somalis in a rowboat. ~~Bullets~~ blankets to Ukraine. A zillion bucks to Paris for .1° Fahrenheit per 100 years. Pallets of cash to Iran so they won't take our milk money. American jobs to illegal aliens until Harrisburg looks like Honduras. The Country's GNP straight to China. Give it all up!" -Obama/Biden

"Hey Moe! Let's do that again! Vote HARR1S/Biden! Yeah, that's it!" -any Lib-ral

---

THE HORN OF EAST AFRICA BLOWS

You are crew on a 1,000' tanker with 26+ feet of freeboard, loaded. 'Long come six skinnies in a 16' skiff. Your corporate geniuses order you to lock yourselves in a "safe room" (Sounds like college. -Editrix) and surrender the ship rather than suffer the skipper to ship a shotgun. If this makes sense to you, please vote Democrat.

Note: Allow us to Trumpet a Solution.

6 skinnies shinnying up six meters of sisal

- 9 blue whistlers per 00 Buck shotgun shell @ 1600 fps*

= 0 times they try this again '

* That's nine .32 caliber lead balls comin' atcha at 1600 feet per second.

Dumbass.

Q: Isn't that racism?

A: Arithmetic.

THEOLOGY (THE DOG WAS AN ASSET. ARE YOU?)

The cow dog was hard on prowlers, easy on visitors. She could spot a deadbeat a block away; was pleasant to any working person. She asked for nothing; gave everything. She had no vices. Since she bore no original sin (that deacon's dodge for every evil), I struggle with her suffering on her final days before we ended it. I accept the death but not the pain. "Does anyone know where the love of God goes?"* She had no vices.

*Gordon Lightfoot

MORE CNN MANTRA

Q: When is a 6'3", 240 lb. man morbidly obese/morbidly obese/morbidly obese?

A: When he is Donald Trump.

Note: Caught by statistics, it's now clinically obese/clinically obese/clinically obese.

Q: Can you say "morbidly obese" and "Michael Moore" in a sentence?

A: Not if you work for CNN.

Q: Can you say "E-mails" to Joe or Hunter?

A: Not if you want to keep working for CNN.

HIBERNATION

The Holy Spirit returned from 2000 years on Capistrano and told Papa Francisco to STFU. -Philberto Excommunicatio

FAKE NEWS BY INNUENDO

10/21/20: ABC News 27 (Channel 5 in Tallahassee) aired, "Thugs at the polls told people they would be beaten up if they did not vote for Trump". (How would they know?) "Law enforcement was notified..." No back-up to the story.

Pure insinuation.

10/22/20: Same station. "A woman said a man said (swear to God) there will be bloodshed if Biden is elected. Law enforcement has been notified, etc."

I guess they figured out the "How would they know?" part. Again, zero back-up.

PS: daytime TV on this channel is replete with Biden ads, most blatantly false to any informed voter. "The Party of the Working Man" knows who sits on their asses all day long. So Vote Biden: Keep 'Em There While You Bust Your Butt Working For A Living. Dumbass. (See? There is an honest Biden ad.)

Note: When BLM thugs in black fatigues carried black clubs within 26' of several polling places, "law enforcement" was not notified and ABC/DNC had nary a peep.

THE THINKING ~~MAN'S~~ PERSON's NEWS

A fox on Fox knows how to bring out her eyes with very little in the way of makeup. Hope her associates Figure this out.

PS: Remember when men didn't do twinkie Applause?

Note: I once dated a makeup artist who could turn a cobby chick into someone whose shoes you stuffed sawbucks into as she shimmied on your table.

Q: Wassa difference between a stripper you throw money at and one you ask to marry you?

A: 'Bout three drinks.

REGIONAL

Damnyankees roast their peanuts. See: aroma.

Southerners ball they peanuts. See: stank.

Q: Don't damnyankees feed balled peanuts to they hogs?

A: Only win they hite they hogs.

Gillibrand Good-Ole Glossary

ball: boil (sometimes: ball)

hite: hate (occasionally: height)

they: their, they're, there (rarely: they)

whenever: when (You think I am making this up, don't you?)

Editrix: Aw, this mikes perfikt sinse. Win you want to slow you speech, you ay-id extrey syllables; mebbe a hyphen or seeks or tin.

Q: Waa would you want to slow down you speech?

A: Waa, to geeve you more tom for to ball you peanuts, seally.

Q: Ever think about writing a Southern-to-English dictionary?

A: Waa?

AFTER & (YIKES!) BEFORE

Yes, ladies, we lie to you; but we don't wear makeup.

YOU, TOO MIGHT SHOOT YOURSELF IN THE HEAD* AND ROLL YOURSELF IN A RUG

Q: Why is security so tight around Hunter Biden's business associates?

A: Vince Foster, Jeff Epstein and 61 other Clinton cronies kinda set the tone.

Remember Ray Albright? Clinton-appointed coroner Fahmy Malik said his dog ate his head. I believe him. Those Weiner dogs are tough. PS: For the name of the man Malik said shot himself in the chest five (5) times*, ask Wolf Blitzer.

CNN has been sitting on the story for decades.

Oh, and Bill Buford got 4 mouthy Arkansas State Troopers re-assigned to Waco (that would be Texas) where they were sent in first and came out dead. Carl Wilson took a bit longer to get at. CNN? CBS? NBC? NYT? AP? Anyone? Anyone?

*With the wrong hand.

IMPUDENCE MEETS IMPOTENCE: THE UNITED STATES SENATE AT WORK

You are asked (but not required) to testify as to why you censored a story about Biden family corruption. You sit quietly while Senator Cruz hollers at you. He demands answers, gets none.

Q: Then what happens?

A: Nothin'

KNOW YOUR DAYTIME AUDIENCE (HINT: HEAR ME ROAR)

"Can't a girl have a sick day?" -Christiane Amanpour*

Women are tough as men until held accountable for anything; they then instantly become victims of sexism. Att Dr. Phil: Sure the man should help around the house, but so should the woman. You said you'd clean the shower stall to keep the peace. Great. Bet bitch watches Oprah while you do so. Dumbass.

*Imagine the outcry if a smelly man called Hillary a "girl".

MR. & MRS. AMERICA, TURN THEM ALL IN -Diane Feinstein-Berto

You have a mezuzah. Pshaw! I have a cell phone drop box.

CHECK THEM HERE

NO CELL PHONES PAST THIS POINT

FIREARMS WELCOME

Sure, y'all might shoot me, but a phone will really piss me off.

HARD ON IMPOTENCE

They controlled both houses of Congress, but gutlessrepublican never-Trumpers "compromised" with openbordersdemocrats and shot down Kate's Law. Nice and impotent, just the way Bill Kristol likes them. Dumbass

DEMS DEFINE TYRANNY

Trump draws 25,000; Joe gets 250. Democrat Governor limits rallies to, you guessed it, 250.

GUTLESS SECTION (WAS SUPPOSED TO BE ON THE COVER)

The sheeple at the Antioch Harvest Fellowship High Baptist/Medium Methodist Southern Scriptures Church of God in Christ the Nazarene proudly profess their pro-Trumpism by festooning the fence with American flags. "It's a code", spouts the sacrist. "It shows that we're pro-Trump."

"Why not use a Trump sign?", asts Geraldo Berto.

"Uh, that might cause trouble", snivels the sacrist.

Editrix: They have a point on the flags. At Hillary's convention, CNN/DNC dutifully diverted their cameras until the Democrats could scurry out and borrow a bunch from local businesses.

Q: Why not buy them? '

A: Win or lose, why the hell would Hillary want to own an American flag?

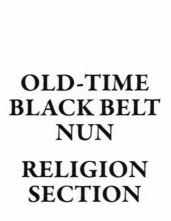

OLD-TIME BLACK BELT NUN

RELIGION SECTION

C HANNELING CHARLTON*
My big, fat book of words (arranged alphabetically) has no moving parts, no buttons or batteries, no power cord, no satellite hook-up. Nevertheless, I managed to learn that Deuteronomy is Greek for "second law ". (Deuce, no?)

It seems that the Law of Moses was laid down twice. Like me, the ancient Hebes were slow learners.

Anyway, a mezuzah contains Deut. 6:4-9 & 11:13-21. I read it and it broke my heart. I thought the thing was simply a profession of one's religion. Turns out, it is a commitment to God's Old Testament Law as put forth by Moses.**

Lucky are they who command that level of faith.

*Aw, everybody knows that Heston wasn't really Moses. He was really Judah Ben-Hur. Wise up. Note: Rumors abound that

Bennie forced a re-take of a chariot race scene when he forgot to remove his wristwatch. Cool.

**When this Law was profoundly abused by the professional prelates of the day, Jesus fired the lot and enacted a New Covenant which is, of course, profoundly abused by the professional prelates of the day.

TARDINESS SECTION (WAS SUPPOSED TO BE ON PAGE ONE)

"They are never, ever ready." -Admiral Lord Nelson

"Arrive last and leave first." -Philberto Gonzalez

The noon Sunday Mass is said in Spanish. It begins at 12:15 because...you know. Still, half the faithful show up at the Gospel*. Meanwhile, someone on cable news felt compelled to report that very few hispanics voted early. !Sorpresa!

*For non- and anti-Catholics, that's 'bout 15 minutes into the service.

Q: If the Mass started at 12:30, when would they show up?

A: Haven't you been paying attention? At the Gospel.

Q: When are they spot on-time?

A: Out the parking lot.**

**Gotta beat them Baptists to the Smokin' Pig.

SCORNED

If you ever start behaving yourself, expect some backlash from the devil. It's going to piss her off.

LIBERAL: SEE "TYRANT"

The Girl Scouts can't celebrate women Supreme Court justices because not all toe the lib-ral line and one was appointed by T-T-Trump. This is the clearest demonstration yet of the danger of democracy and how it invites mob rule. It at once explains the genius of the Electoral College and why the Founders set up a republic, not a democracy. Your tenured hoax will explain the difference after he/she/undecided looks it up, but your grade will suffer for having asked the question. Welcome to the lib-ral world.

UNINFORMED BALLOT, AND MORE TIME TO CAST IT. THANK ANY LIB-RAL.

Early voting didn't give them enough time to drag in the deadbeats who are their constituency; they demand late voting as well. No surprise there. These are the ninnies who support late-term abortion until the moment of birth because bitch can't get her shit together.* If this makes sense to you, please vote Democrat.

*Bruh. She's using abortion as birth control, having somehow evaded eight methods of prevention, and you're expecting a thought process. Hope she never does manage to vote; or breed.

DESPERADO

Even CNN/DNC's crazy camera angles couldn't always hide the fact that Biden was yelling at 20 people per "rally", so they conjured drive-up events. 20 cars take up the space of 200 people and make more noise. C-c-carbon footprint? Where've you been? Consistency is not a lib-ral trait. Ask Al "Five House" Gore when he steps out of his Lear jet. Then vote Democrat. Dumbass.

WELL, THERE GO <u>MY</u> LURID PLEASURES

Oh, sure. Just in case St. Peter's First Epistle General wasn't enough, along comes Charles Stanley with, "...the 'salt' (goodness) we would spread around is diluted by a sinful lifestyle, which also dims the light of our moral authority". Dang! I gotta quit watchin' this guy.

Attention Bible quoters: Never, ever open the Good Book at random. 'Steada, "Good works without faith are filthy rags", you might could get, "Faith absent good works is a clanging gong and a tinkling cymbal", which will muck up your intention of leaving Sunday service as the same old self-righteous prick.

Amen.

THE ARCHBISHOPRIC NOW HARBORS ILLEGALS IN HIS NEIGHBORHOOD...JUST KIDDING*

Catholic Services buys into the "children ripped from their parents' arms" lie, but is hugely silent on the "late-term babies ripped from the womb" fact.

*Next: Archbishopric pays restitution for fugitives' thefts...kidding.

NEWS FLASH FOR YUPPIE TREE HUGGERS WHO
BUY BOUNTY

Porous pages from old phone books/catalogs will wipe
your greasy skillet and start your fire. (Wait for it...) "But...but
then we can't recycle them!"

YUPPIE

Is challenged by p-p-peeling an egg, so he/she/it boils
them in egg-shaped T-T-Tupperware.

11/3/20

One (1) voter fraud case favored Republicans... Oops!
None did.

SAVING THEM SAVES YOU

Feeding my gaggle of angels (and couple imps) I blurted a
Biden and asked the Lord why they hada crap so much. Big picture: helping them helps us. If you doubt this, visit someone
who has only himself to think about.

HER HIPPIE MOM

and ex-hippie grandmom taught her slobbery and the feminists declared it sexist to clean up the mess. 'Lessen you want
your place lookin' like Woodstock, Occupied Wall Street or
any Earth Day celebration, you'd better check out...

BACKFIRE

MTV/TEEN MORON MOMS wanted us to Vote
For Our Lives. Realizing that we are 1,000 times
more at risk from Thug Michael Brown & Thief
Trayvon Martin, we did.
Getting them counted was another matter.

HARRIET, I MEAN,

HARRY HOMEMAKER SECTION

A NOSE IS A NOSE

You knew a nettie pot is stupid just by the name. Sounds like "macrame" or "Birkenstock" or "Vespa". Real cutting-edge stuff. Oh, and the electric pump contraption (Hope it never shorts out!) is like dragging out a Dyson 'counta you don't own a b-b-broom. All's you need to spiff-up you sinuses is a NeilMed squeeze bottle. Comes with pre-measured hits o' saline fixin's. Kumbaya.

SINK STINK

She shoved spaghetti-ohs* down it 'till the drain plugged up and your sink plunger is next door. Before you go all girlie** on it: fill it halfway and upend a half-liter bottle of water inta the drain. Push the bottom down hard and fast, like an accor-

46

dion in heat. The slug of uncompressible water will push the plug-up past the p-trap, pronto. Note: Cutting off the bottle neck gives a better seal, faster flush. PS: A sink plunger is 3 bucks. Tell the neighbor to buy his own.

*To make pasta, she'd have to b-b-boil water.

**All girlie: Hug tree. Dump chemicals in drain.

Hug tree. Throw out rags, buy Bounty.

Hug tree, Throw out b-b-broom, buy Bissel.

Hug tree, Buy Yoplait yogurt in cutesy backwards containers that entrap baby skunks, squirrels, etc, and kill them slowly by strangulation and/or suffocation.

GO "Aww!" every time you see the film. Kumbaya.

ATT LEFTISTS:

The end justifies the means. -Karl Marx.

If your cause is just you don't have to lie about it. -Phil Berto

No one "pushes" drugs. If you have good shit, people come to you. -Chris Rock

If you have the good of the people/planet at heart, why are you so vicious? A worthy concept needs no hard sell, no riot, no on-fire po-lice cars. If what you offer is wonderful, people will steal it. Dumbass.

BIDEN IMMEDIATELY ASSEMBLED his information po-lice: called Trump a dictator for wanting a fair vote count.

BACKYARD FISHPOND

Skim it in the morning while the poop "worms" are floating. By noon they'll sink and defy removal. Don't sweat what you miss; fish don't need a sterile environment; as usual, a balance is best. Your best defense against ammonia, which kills oxygen, is aeration. Any small fountain will do, especially if it has a filter.

If you want fish you can see (Who doesn't?), buy some "feeder" goldfish.* Then eat the fish that would eat your goldfish. Note: Yuppies will ignore the 25¢ goldfish and insist on coi.

Q: Wassa difference 'tween a goldfish and a coi?

A: 'Bout $29. But then you can say, "So, I have a coi pond?"

PS: Feed your 2", 25¢ goldfish crushed pellets 'till they double in size (couple weeks if you add some duckweed from the nearest swamp). Once they're bluegill size (couple months), stop the duckweed or you'll have a pondful o' footballs a/k/a/ carp.**

*Goldfish are rarely as variegated as coi. Moreover, they lose their individuality over time (So, goldfish are lib-rals?) and obediently settle on the standard orange. Onna plus side, their working-class livery produces a deeper, brighter orange than any coi, and you just saved $172.50 on six fish (You're welcome), so Get Over It.

**l was struck by how similar a carp is to a Blue Marlin the day I saw Michelle slouching next to Melania.

Next: A square, white, $250 box (scratch & dent: $158) that lasts 30 years and cleans, really cleans your clothes vs. a custom-color designer edifice that claims to do 25 pounds of laundry with a quart of water (with predictable results) which you'll be making payments on. You might could be a yuppie if you chose the latter and placed it on the second floor. What's that? It threw a hose? Dumbass.

SOCIALISM 101

Within days of his election (so-called), Biden set up an agency (Surprise!) to control access to information (Surprise!) staffed by his cronies in Big Tech (Surprise!) who had censored the New York Post articles about Hunter's collusion* with China and Russia. The concept of budding bullshit bureaucracies to enact crap that could never, ever be passed by the people's representatives (so-called) in Congress is The Way of the left. This is more thoroughly (and elegantly) handled by Laura Ingraham in <u>Billionaire At The Barricades</u>.

*Every single thing that Adam Schiff accused Trump of had already been done by Hunter & Hillary. "Accuse the opposition of <u>your</u> malfeasance." -Socialism 101

"DOES ANYONE KNOW WHERE THE LOVE OF GOD GOES..." -Gordon Lightfoot

By arrangement, the old gentleman carried the cat in his arms through the waiting room into the treatment area, followed closely by his wife. The scene was the sadder because kitty was alert; her bright eyes missed nothing. It was her little body that was worn out. The Lord was kinder to me in that the inverse is true. Still I wonder: what was that sweet cat's original sin?

How Doc does this every day I'll never know.

FOLKS EITHER LOVE OR HATE MY NEW YARD
SIGN.
<u>DEAD? VOTE BIDEN.</u>
Bumper stickers are on order.

STORM

The gutters are cleared, the brush pile is burned off, the
firewood is in, the animals are barned on fresh bedding. Let 'er
rain!

"Be prepared." We learned that in Boy Scouts. You remember them; the finest youth program on the planet. 'Long come
the forerunners of the LGBTQ-WHATEVER thugs. Sneaky
bastards. Set out to fuck it all up. And they did.

"Let us be scoutmasters or we'll sue", threatened the queers,
knowing that our liberal-compliant gov-mint bureaucrats
would back them. So We The Sheeple, products of the aging
hippie kumbaya crowd, weakly complied. "Hell, 'they' say that
pedophiles are always straight men." HUH? If-they-were-
straight-they-would-not-molest-boys, you fucking moron.

The BSA was sued into bankruptcy by, you guessed it, boys
who were molested by queer scoutmasters. Surprise! You fucking moron.

Editrix: Wanna fuck something up? Count on our unelect-
ed, unaccountable, unremoveable sociology degree career gov-
mint bureaucrats to assist.

PS: Aw, don't sell that sociology degree in nothingness short. If you get fired from your dishwashing job, you can always teach.

BY THE BALLS

Q: How would Biden negotiate with China?

A: Hat in hand.

Q: What would Biden give China to keep Hunter out of jail?

A: Anything they want.

HARDON

We've been kinda har...tough on Steele Brim lately. In his defense, his job depends on obedience to the role MTV/ TEEN MORON MOMS has set for him. Smart.

FISHY

The Carp to Melania's Blue Marlin lectured the half of the Country that didn't riot about "unity". Translation: Shut up and accept voter fraud.

No thanks, Michelle.

MEDIA MATTERS AND LIB-RALS ARE EASY

If BLM Marxists could make thug Michael Brown, who tried to murder a cop with his own gun, a hero of our lib-ral useful idiots with nothing more than the "Hands up, don't shoot" lie, well, foisting a cute EMT whose boyfriend shot a cop should be a piece of cake. Thanks to CNN/DNC, it was.

ELECTION

Even with all the fraud favoring Biden, Trump won despite the best efforts of both Parties. Lessee if we can keep our President in spite of it/them.

TO COVER HER LYIN' ASS

The CNN reportrix said, "We 'heard' that Trump supported the violence". Do-dah.

VOTES VS VIEWERSHIP

Thank you, Fox News, for the tiny story about a van in a parking lot. May we now look forward to something on, say, SMARTMATIC/DOMINION?

DO THE MATH

Tens of thousands showed up at every Trump rally. Tens of...well, ten attended the typical Biden bash. CNN's clever camera angles could not hide the fact that few saw Biden as a viable candidate. Turns out, he wasn't.

Pray that facts will overcome the liberal establishment and its deep state/big media/big tech/big bank/big teacher/big pharma/big labor allies. Pray.

OUR BODIES, OURSELVES

We will commit partial-birth infanticide whenever we choose and call it a women's health issue. What? Only 10 at Thanksgiving? Cancel Christmas? Uh, OK. If that's what President-elect Joekammy (Joke-a-me) wants. Hear me roar.

EYE BALLS

Every optometrist (and DMV) office on the planet uses the same eye chart. (You think I am making this up, don't you?) The last two lines you need to see to be deemed 20-20 are felopcid and devpotec. (Say, "fel-op-cid" and "dev-po-tec". There, you'll never forget them.) Hot Tip: Do not "read" them too fast or the bitch will make you say them backwards. Oops!

THEIRS & MINE

The BLM school indoctrination video shows genius Michael Brown as a fresh-faced kid in a graduation cap. Tee-hee.

My security camera footage shows thug Michael Brown shoving a small South Korean store owner and stealing a cigar.

N.B.: Their cartoon teaches youngsters how to be victims; my actual footage shows oldsters how not to.

LIB-RAL LOGIC

11/14/2020. BLM thugs attacked stragglers from a MA-GA rally. This got "reported" as white supremacist aggression. Follow the lib-ral logic. MAGA folks are often accused of racism by the media; I guess they attacked themselves. Trump, of course, was said to have "condoned this violence" against his own supporters. By his own supporters. Note: Half the population believe this madness, proving that the dumb-down has worked. Thank a teacher.

DUMB & DUMBER

In our so-called democracy, populists are outnumbered by big-govmint aficionados. Thank a teacher.

DOMINION

Fox News: "Unless something big happens..." Huh. It IS happening. How 'bout reporting it?

PANTS ON FIRE (NOW SAY 10 HAIL MARYS AND MAKE A GOOD ACT OF CONTRITION)

11/15/2028: Faux-elect Biden says he "spoke with the Holy Father". Yeah, right. About what, Joe? Picture Papa Francisco saying, "Sure, Joseph, I'll support having American tax-payers foot the bill for some deadbeat's late-term/partial-birth infanticide, 'slong as you let Catholic Services continue to harbor unvetted, unvaccinated, unemployed illegal alien invaders in other people's neighborhoods. Mama mia, I almosta forgotta: Ya gotta turn Trump's wall into bridges over the Rio Grande. My wall? Hell, Son, I'ma keepa my wall."

Note: It sounds funnier in Latin: "Valium Trumpum delenda est". Ha, ha!

BUREAUCRAT APPRENTICE

Call the Tallahassee Capitol switchboard and hear young snotty say, "The Welcome Center is closed". OK, I didn't want an explanation, but a clue as to when the "Welcome Center" will he able to take and re-route calls would have been helpful. Imagine private industry doing this during normal hours.

PS: Half of our dumbed-down (thank a teacher) population will vote for more big gov-mint bureaucracy, every time. Dumbass.

ALL ANIMALS ARE STRICTLY DRY; THEY SINLESS LIVE AND EARLY DIE.

They own no original sin, so why do they suffer so? -Padre Berto

We expect cheetahs to handle well; they use that long tail as a rudder.

Lions corner by sheer strength of will. Hope you brought enough gun.

Att yuppies: lose your whistle, quick. It might upset his stomach.**)

** On a smaller scale: took in an injured tomcat. While he was in for repairs, Doc took his testes, so he should have calmed down. He didn't. Soon's he mended he thought he'd bully the others. Think again. Up steps little Ethne*, half his size and twice as tough. She slaps his face and convinces him that it is in his best interest to behave. Att parent/friends: R U listening?

*Jacked-up rear end, tufts on her ears, stub for a tail: part Bobcat. Badass.

DENNY'S

Server 1: I'm off at midnight. Hope there's no post-election violence.

Server 2: If you talk about my people like that I'll unfriend you.

Server 1: Late. My friends sometimes talk shit, but never in yuppiespeak.

PS: I never said "your people" are violent, but you just did.

WASTE NOT, EAT WELL

Having seen fire fighterettes throw out the roast beef drippings and open a jar of "gravy" because that's what their ex-hippie moms did, not much surprises me, but The Girl had to be told to save the leftover stew. This I heated, topped each serving with a runny egg, and had it for breakfast.

With the New Girl.

MOM SAID POACHED IS HEALTHIER

So I float eggs in bacon grease. Spooning some on top cooks 'em faster. Where's my nitro?

LIB-RALS R EASY

If BLM Marxists could make pig-faced thug Michael Brown, who tried to murder a cop with his own gun, a hero of the useful idiots with the "Hands up, don't shoot" lie, why, foisting a cute EMT whose boyfriend shot a po-lice would be a piece of cake. Thanks to our liberal-compliant "news" media, it was.

PLANET PREVAILS OVER PROGRESSIVES

I was glum when British Petroleum spilled millions of barrels of oil into the Gulf. As toxic as crude petroleum is, the Good Lord has provided a microorganism that eats the stuff. The Earth's self-cleansing mechanisms are amazing. The Planet even recovered from the unspeakable filth left behind at Woodstock, The Isle of Wight, any Earth Day "celebration" (piss & shit fest); even the trash tossed by A Million Mengele Moms For Late-Term Infanticide finally went away at, of course, taxpayer expense. Thus, I believe that sunlight UV rays and time will break down irresponsibly discarded plastic if we limit its use and stop importing folks whose response to "Please Don't Litter" is, "¿Que?".

Note: Next time some yuppie tsk-tsks your water bottle, ask her how many cans she washes out and smashes flat before recycling them. Ditto that cutesy backwards container/animal trap she eats her Yoplait Yogurt from, designed just for her.

Editrix: Hey, she cares. Each and every time she sees footage of a baby skunk, squirrel, etc. slowly suffocating to death, she will murmur, "Awww!".

Hear me roar.

PERSPECTIVE (IMAGINE THIS, DO-DA-DO)

Q: Can you IMAGINE the smell when all those dinosaurs died at once?

A: So, like Woodstock? S-S-San F-F-Francisco? Christiane Amanpour's car?

PS: The Planet is cleansing itself of those shitfests; it'll handle Antifa.

FINE CUSWEEN

Ast a Southern gal to bring home some garlic, you'll get something in a jar or bottle. They don't be no pastrami 'counta they don't be no pork innit.

Note: She will also bring Lucky Charms, Front Loops or Cocoa Puffs.

Q: For the kids?

A: For her seff. (Kinda explains her tooth problem.}

Q: She has trouble with her teeth?

A: Tooth.

FIRST, DO NO HARM

Dr. Ernesto "Che" Guevara was the first to volunteer whenever Fidel needed someone executed. Useful idiots put his starry-eyed likeness on their T-shirts.

My favorite fotographia was released by the Bolivian government. 'Egualmente'.

PS: Che whinnied, "I'm worth more to you alive than dead". Si, Senor. Pa-chow!

GILLIBRAND GLOSSARY

Southerner on a bicycle: see DUI

47 YEARS OF TALKIN'

First debate: Biden wanted Trump to say, "Law & Order with Safety". Joe didn't know that Trump signed the Safe Policing For Safe Communities Executive Order on June 16. Why, next thing you know, Joe will suggest criminal justice reform...

Oops! Keep talkin', Scooter.

Debate 1 should have been a blowout, but it changed nary a vote. Three times Joe was headed down that rabbit hole, only to be saved by Trump's interruption. Best way to beat Biden is to let him speak.

PUSSY POWER

Venetian blind blocking the cat's view? Relax. She will remove the appropriate slats.

COMMON COLD MEETS SHITFEST

Today's sanctity of motherhood slings her sick spawn into daycare, preschool or elementary/middle/high child warehousing without a thought about spreading the joy. You expect her to stay home to care for he/she/it? Tee-hee. She has her feminist-mandated job to go to. She is allowed to be a breeder; she is not permitted to act like one. Anyway, her "unemployed at the moment" man-bun boyfriend and/or "wife" can handle those chores. Advantage: "progressives".

PS: A low-grade bacterial/viral infection will set you up for something stronger, so cancel your visit to any sanctuary city. Be advised that "San Francisco" is Spanish for "Shit On The Sidewalk". Look it up.

Yuppie Alert: I believe they still evaporate "sea salt" in San Francisco Bay.

PS: San Francisco Bay: receptacle of the effluent of San Jose, Oakland, Alameda, etc. Home of several Navy yards, where you can watch them sandblast anti-fouling paint off slimy ship hulls. Bilgewater is the nicest thing gets dumped there.

PS: Kinda 'splains why yuppies make such good Antifa fodder. They enjoy being sought-after as useful idiots of the left.

IMAGINE THERE'S NO COUNTRY...(TRANSLATION: NO MONEY, FOOD, FREEDOM. ASSHOLE.)

Obedient lib-rals everywhere advised us to avoid Goya food products over some politically-correct bullshit or other, so I bought a bunch of Goya food products. Turns out, Goya food products are a cut above the stuff* I had been buying. I now enjoy top-quality Goya food products and get to support a family-owned business while I'm attit. Thanks, thought police!

*I compared labels. The organic black beans I was using contained "sea" salt.

PS: Goya food products' founder is an immigrant. Imagine that (do-da-do). Asshole.

THE 4 STAGES OF LIFE

Youth, middle-age, "you look good", and your socks don't match.

PS: Somewhere between the last two, your crotch quits. Do-dah.

GIVE IT AWAY

Mongol hordes conquered countries. American sheeple elected AOC, Rashida Tlaib & Ilhan Omar.

PAVING THE PLANET, TWO FEET AT A TIME

No one has tried harder to save the Earth than Birkenstock. In case your hairy legs & pits don't stifle a suitor, why, just strap your dirty dogs into a pair of horse harness horrors to make yourself undoable. Sure, Laura Ashley really tried, but only Birkenstock made a dent in Teen Moron Moms and even stopped a few semi-responsible knock-ups. The system was working until the Woodstock generation switched from weed to heroin, which enabled them to do anything to anyone, including chicks with hoofs that looked like canal boats.

Some of these smellies sought sociology and statistics degrees in nothingness and, after serving an apprenticeship flippin' burgers, became teachers; but the brighter Birkenstock broads and the losers who got themselves high enough to hit them simply signed-up for gov-mint assistance and bought Hanoi Jane exercise videos, knowing that she had ~~manned~~ personned a North Vietnamese anti-aircraft gun and pretended to shoot down their fathers, brothers and sons.

Three generations of this shit and Antifa/BLM Marxixts now have to turn away some of these useful idiots for want of enough black Fascist shirts, black Isis flags, black Matters clubs, and lunch money.

Birkenstock's efforts were doomed to failure. For all their whining about overpopulation, the ex-hippie know nothings and the ~~students~~ attendees they ~~taught~~ indoctrinated began to encourage open borders. They simply replaced a glut of American-born babies with an overflow of unvaccinated urchins whelped by unvetted, unemployed, illegal alien invaders whose response to, "Please don't throw diapers out the car window", is, "?Que?".

Look for logic elsewhere. Kumbaya.

JOE WILL ADD TO 47 YEARS OF TALK AND CORRUPTION
"We will bury you!" -Nikita Kruschev

"We'll do it ourselves." -The American Sheeple

When DNC/AOC/BLM/ANTIFA bankrupt the Country, gov-mint services will suffer.

Q: Will my kids still get they own "free" cell phones at taxpayer expense?

A: They'll hafta share.

Q: Even the two with the same last name?

A: Find they baby daddy.

NOT AMY VANDERBILT

The wimpy wine steward likes making a show of circumcising the seal before removing the cork. Ruin young snotty's day: take out your Buck knife, slit the seal, and remove the sumbitch. Unless, of course, you like your wine poured over the freshly-cut edge of lead foil. Do-dah.

NOT ANY NAME

Gotta feel for any chick named "Melodi". They know, they fucking know, that their parents had low expectations for them.

Options for anyone named "Melodi": cult member, seeds & stems shoppe owner, tree hugger, palm reader, pole dancer, sociologist, NEA teacher, Democrat.

TRUMP DISAVOWED KKK, etc.; Obama/Biden embraced Farrakan and Rev. Wright.

LOST SKILLSET

The quality is just OK, but the concept is sound. You bring home a can of "condensed" soup (half the weight) and add a can of water as you heat it.

Yuppie broad: So, you...you-have-to-add-water?

Her director: A can for every can.

Yuppie broad: So, I guess I can do that? Alexa! So, put 347 ml in the soup?

Any feminist: Atta girl!

Yuppie broad: So, hear me roar?

OUT OF AFRICA

Robert Redford does a good job playing a man who can shoot a lion at close range and avoid doing the some when it is unnecessary. His big-bore double rifle does not make lever-action noises, so Hollywood finally had someone on set who knew something about guns. The only glitch in this beautifully photographed film was when Mr. Redford pitched a tent. He grabbed a manly mallet and actually took aim at a stake as if he was lining up a half-mile sniper shot. The great white hunter then proceeded to tap-tap-tap his target like any 5 year-old. It was obvious that Redford had never held, much less used, a hammer. Leading Lady Meryl Streep was, of course, flawless.

Gillibrand Glossary

Hollywood: thinks all guns, including singles, doubles, bolt actions, semi-autos & revolvers go "shick-shick" when chambering a round.

muzzle-loading rifle: even in Hollywood, the smokepole doesn't go "shick-shick".

lib-ral: trades his granddad's Parker shotgun for some weed.

progressive: breaks granddad's Parker smashing a car window to save the Planet.

BLM: steals your granddad's Parker, breaks it smashing a window to get sneakers.

ANTIFA: steals your granddad's Parker, points it at you and makes you say, "black lives matter".

DEMOCRAT: Party of the Workingman if the workingman has never hammered a nail,

fired a gun, or spent his own money. Approves all of the above until polls dictate otherwise.

ANY DEMOCRAT

I was up all night thinking of ways to spend Other People's Money. How 'bout: an old lady could fall down the stairs and need a phone. Why not start a program (on the backs of the taxpayers, of course) that gives her a "free" phone?

Phone Company: I like it!

$enator $ubsidy: #Me too?

Suppose her grandkids lose their "free" bus pass and have to w-w-walk to the vape/tattoo/piercing/nail salon? Teens need phones, too.For...uh...safety.

Yikes! The younger kids! If they miss the school bus, they ain't allowed to wake their sanctity of motherhood. She's been sleeping 'till Oprah ever since the gov-mint told her the school would make a sammich (lunch) and pour some Froot Loops in-na bowl (breakfast) on the backs of the taxpayers. Hell, it went on all summer. PS: Mom serenely sleeps-in knowing every mistake has its phone.

Editrix: If any of this makes any sense to you, please keep votin' Democrat.

FUCK
HOLLYWOOD

Dwayne Johnson could have kept his pride and still worked by starting his own production company.

SO, GALA YUPPIE SECTION?

#######

C HRIS DON'T ROCK NO MORE
       He cleaned up his act and instantly lost his sense of timing and humor. Struggling now, he took a cheap shot at a man (Trump) with a life-threatening illness (covid), wishing the latter to prevail. Tired.

Confidential to Chris Rock: Your heart can't go out to covid. Yon handed that organ to the establishment the day you professed obedience to political correctness. Oh, and while you were attit, they also took your balls.

Editrix (in yuppiespeak): "So, the heroes of the left evoke unfunny political "humor"? So, Kimmel, Mahr and Rock have all been turned on by the thought police? So, rather than fight back (With what? See paragraph 2. Ed.), they all suck up? So, none have ever saved a life nor taken one in defense of someone? So, they would make lousy first responders or ranchers; but excellent sociologists?"

Q: So, what does a person with a sociology degree DO?
A: So, flip burgers?
Note: Kimmel obediently did a sick skit about dying Charlton Heston. Lib-rals won't recall that Heston marched

for civil rights in Selma long before Hollywood elites thought it was cool. Heston's crime was his defense of your right to d-d-defend yourself...Aw, it's over your head.

Q: So, that's what the police are for?

A: So, the police you defunded? (consistency is not a lib-ral trait)

Hot Tip: The very best po-lice take a minute or three to respond; kinda long when you are under attack...like I said: It's over your head.

Q: So, does "over your head" mean Antifa is clubbing you?

A: So, Jimmy and Bill and Chris would apparently wish it so?

Editrix: Aw, any compassionate open-borders lib-ral would wish it so.

Final Note: Kimmel was given a tour of the Everglades by buncha good ol' boys who remained gracious even as this hapless human openly mocked them. Then, just in case you hadn't noticed what an ass he is, Jimmy pointed a shotgun at the camera(man). Kimmel may never have saved a life or taken one in defense of someone as helpless as himself, but he is a shoe-in for the "I Didn't Know It Was Loaded Fool" trophy. Damn dumbass.

Final Note (Swear to God): So, Chris Rock's stand-up was a hit in D.C., where they work? So, it flopped in Oakland, where they don't? So, the old Chris knew the difference between working folks (of every color) and deadbeats (of every color)? So, no lib-ral will tolerate this?

DOCTOR VS SAINT

So, she sees more patients in a day than any doctor? So, she has her learned Staff follow-up on every one? So, her charges can't say where it hurts? So, she has to know her shit?

Q: So, if it wouldn't nix her license, would you ask your vet to do your bypass?

A: So, I already did?

EYES

"Melania looks like she's about to sneeze." -NYT toad

"You may not mention Michelle's." - Any lib-ral

SOCIOLOGY. STATISTICS. POLY-SCI. BULL-SHIT.

People do attend college to become teachers. I know them both. The rest find out that they took on a 20-year debt for a degree in nothingness. Cum laude.

Q: What will they do when they tire of flippin' burgers?

A: Teach.

THE MOST MISUSED WORD IN JOURNALISM IS "JOURNALISM"

Pence: where do you stand on packing the Supreme Court?

Harris: Gbdox mfplrj spohxd felopcid devpotec.

CNN: Pence picked on a woman. Hear me roar.

Press: Where do you stand on packing the Supreme Court?

Biden: I'll answer after the election.

CNN: Trump is not transparent.

Press: What's in the Obamacare bill?

Nancy: We'll find out after we pass it.

CNN: Trump is not transparent.

* Rules of the new 'journalism': 1-unseat Trump. 2-Cover Kammy. 3-Never, ever get downwind of Christiane Amanpour.

DE BAIT

Most would be nervous about debating Mike Pence. Not so Kamala Harris. Her flawless smile flashed throughout the proceedings, and it scared the crap outta me. I was reminded of Barack Obama's winsome ways, and how genuine his grin seemed. I had voted otherwise, but I was not unpleased to have him as our President. Until Benghazi. Suddenly, the depth of the corruption of Hillary's State Department and, by extension, Obama's administration, was evident even before that regime's involvement in the Russia collusion hoax came out.

Kammy's canned smile covers her intentions; not so with Michelle, whose vitriolic video exposes the pure hatred in those reptilian* eyes. Our "Permanent First Lady" (her words) spat out a speech that made it clear: America pisses her off. Period. Half of our people disgust her. Just as she was never proud of her... Excuse me... your Country until it elected her husband, she has now decreed that you are a racist if you fail to vote as she tells you to.

Dear Michelle: You hate me and half my countrymen from your $27 million home on Martha's Vineyard. You're welcome.

PS: How 'bout couple windmills out front of that breezy island?

PS: Steelo Brim loves to point out haters. 100% he lets this one go.

Q: Commitment?

A: Obedience.

Q: And Rob Dyrdek?

A: Busy founding Parents For Pushing Pot.

* I told a lib-ral that Michelle's feral eyes reminded me of a caged animal at the Bronx Zoo. "That's so racist", she whinnied. Turns out, while I was thinkin' reptilian, her first thought was "simian". Oh, but I'm the racist.

YEARS OF PRACTICE

Q: Why are women better actors than men?

A: They've been fooling mirrors all their lives.

IMAGINE THAT

"We're going to have a long, dark winter" didn't work with conservatives. Who knew?

IT IS EVERYWHERE

As a Life Member of the NRA (Oh, shit! Doxxed and listed!), I've sent lotsa donations over the years. This faux-election cycle I did not see one TV ad in North Florida. Not one.

Questions or comments? This is not your father's NRA. You'll get to buck a bureaucracy of yuppies that would make any grotesque gov-mint agency proud.

RESISTANCE TO WHAT?

So, they feel badass while texting each other from across the room?

They call themselves the "resistance" while being duped into opposing a Washington outsider who fights big pharma, big labor and big banks.

They fancy themselves avant garde even as they are manipulated by big media and big tech.

They consider themselves intellectual elites after cowing to tenured hoaxes who mindlessly peddle socialism.

They are exactly what one would expect after three generations of ex-hippie parent/friending and liberal NEA (union, no competency testing) teachers. I did not write the Resistance Relativity Index; they did.

Resistance Relativity Index

Capitalist drives Royce: conspicuous consumption (now: white privilege)

Cardi B drives Rolls (new money always says, "Rolls"): eat your heart out

Wave gun at Trump supporters: good

Defend self, home, kids, store: bad

"Baby it's cold outside": pro-rape

"Beat it up nigga! WAP!": so cool!

The pillage of Portland: summer of love

The sacking of Seattle: mostly peaceful protest

Looting and vandalism: mostly peaceful protest

All lives matter: white supremacist dogwhistle

Late-term/partial-birth abortion: choice

School vouchers/school choice: selfish and (now) illegal

Taxpayer-paid abortion on demand: women's health issue

WHY THE FOUNDERS SET UP A REPUBLIC

Democracy is insane. Look around you. Half of what you see should not drive or breed, much less vote.

Editrix: They didn't. Democrat operatives "voted" for them.

FISH DON'T KNOW THEY'RE WET. FISH ARE LIB-RALS.

Conservatives often mix with non-conservatives. They perceive that people exist with d-d-differences of opinion; that there actually can be d-d-diversity of thought.

Guest Editorial: What? Diversity means skin color, you racist. -Obedient Lib-ral

REMINDS ME: REINCARNATION: God's gift to fools.

BLESS US, OH LORD, AND THESE THY GIFTS...

Binge eating lately? View a holocaust documentary. You'll suddenly appreciate a sensible meal.

THE "M" WORD

Talkin' to MSDNC, you may not point to the mob that is looting your store. You may mention the mostly peaceful protesters who are re-distributing your wealth.

WHAT A GUY!

CNN's hero this week is a delivery ~~man~~ person who, while on his route, takes orders from upper, upper middle-class broads who are (supposedly) scared to shop 'counta covid. They answer the door in Gucci and Rolex to place their orders for Silk Almond Milk, organic baby carrots, Belgian truffles...you think I am making this up, don't you? PS: see, BLESS US, OH LORD...

CHANTING NEWS NETWORK (LOOKIT THE RIOTS: LIB-RALS LOVE THEIR CHANTS)

2 years: Nam myoho collusion kyo.

6 months: Nam Ukraine renge kyo.

forever; Nam myoho renge corona.

hoping for more: 200,000*, 200,000*, 200,000*

*95 year-old smoker's heart infarcts, tests positive. CNN: died of covid.

*plane crashes, mixed charred remains test positive: CNN: died of covid.

*man bisected in car crash, covid under his toenail. CNN: died of covid.

*San Francisco bum dies of hepatitis, tent tests ++. CNN: died of covid.

Translation: 50,000 covid deaths plus 150,000 other causes, covid in the area.

Do-dah.

BUT...BUT HE WORE GLOVES...

The yuppie broad scolds you for not wearing a mask in your yard, then buys broccoli, melon, etc. already cut up. I guess she never saw the footage of the illegal food worker scratching his ass with his knife. Bon appétit.

MORE LIB-RAL LOGIC ("THE GUN IS FOR P-PRO... SAFETY" -Kammy)

The system is corrupt. Elect a man who has been part of it for 47 years.

PS: His running mate smoked weed with a gun in the car while driving home from a day of prosecuting folks for smoking weed with a gun in the car.

EMOTION VS FACTS

"We will invest in schools and health care." -Harris/Biden

"Yay!" -any progressive

"How?" -any conservative

REALTOR LINGO

Charming: Needs work. Lotsa work.

Fixer-upper: Burn it down and start over.

DEEP STATE: WE MUST FOLLOW THE "SCIENCE".
OBEDIENT LIB-RAL: O.K.

Lockdowns don't work; the virus awaits when you come out.

Herd immunity works if you don't lock down.

We must have lock downs.

Q: How does that "follow the science"?

A: Doesn't. We just say that to get you to accept control. Get used to it.

Note: .2% of school kids get covid.

Cuomo & DeBlasio: Close the schools!

Obedient Lib-ral: O.K.

ASK FAUCI

Masks don't help. You probably should wear a mask. If you can. Then you should felopcid, but only after you devpotec. (I get paid for this shit!)

ALIENS

Whatever planet cats are from must be 40-60°F. That's when my goofies are at their best.

Note: Keep your unwanted guest room just so. Visits will be short.

COMPROMISE WITH COMMUNISTS

I think Trump won. My neighbor thinks Biden won. Nobody will ever know. Fox No News may downplay it all day long, but it's not supposed to be that way.

BIDENPUMPKIN

Pumpkins are a low-tech cash crop well suited to small farmers. Chestnut Hill Foods, distributed by Midwood Brands, Blue State Virginia knows this, and they support said small farmers. In China. The penny a can they saved (pumpkin is cheap) cost them, and the stores that stock their communist crap, a customer.

PS: Unless you like your food sourced in (yuppie for "from") covid-infested* fields, you may want to Read The Label.

*Aw, the W.H.O., which Biden wants us back into, accepts China's "data" on covid: 1 case in Beijing, 3 cases in Bum-fuk. Bon appetit.

1776 NEW WORLD ORDER 1776

To promote prosperity and peace, your Country was founded on the principle of economic independence, which in turn brought political independence. Sound unfamiliar? Of course it does. Thank your tenured hoax Marxist professor. Then ask (approved pronoun) why July 4th is called "Independence Day". Dumbass.

LOOSIN' TEETH: I NOW floss with a rope.

ATT FOX NEWS: NOW THAT Trump has spilled the beans on Dominion, maybe Mrs. Murdoch will let you report it.

IT IS A WONDERFUL COUNTRY IF YOU CAN KEEP IT. -Benjamin Berto

"We have met the enemy, and they are us." -Al Capp

"I hope not." (Don't doxx me, Bro.) -P. Phantomini

Democracy: Worked well in ancient Greek city-states where citizens shared a common language and culture.

Republic: Effective in large, diverse countries where people work for a living and contribute <u>something</u> to society.

Mob Rule: This shit happens when 51% are on the dole. Parasites must vote Democrat to "keep their shit coming" because they are lazy. They are easy to control via Big Media & Big Tech because they are stupid. This is what passes for "democracy" today.

Dictatorship: Cures all of the above. Scary but necessary when half the population has been dumbed-down.

Strong Presidency: Splits the difference. Men like Washington, Jefferson and Reagan were strong Presidents leading a strong Country run by the people. Persons like Carter, Obama and Obiden were weak politicians presiding over a flaccid country run by the United Nations and Big Media as overseen by Big Tech.

IRONY

Trump is accused of dictatorship for enforcing the votes of the people. Meanwhile, JoeKammy speak of punishing the opposition and suppressing diversity of opinion before their "election" is even settled. See: dumbed-down dictionary.

Choice: Means abortion. Period. All other choice (school, etc.) is banned.

Diversity: Skin. Period. All other diversity (thought, opinion) is banned.

IRONY II

The real dictatorship is Big-Everything (Media, Tech, Teaching, Farmer, Labor, etc.) seizing a crisis (Covid) to permit mail-in ballots and prevent poll watching in order to install a puppet regime that China <u>owns</u>.

IRONY III

Just as the Joke-a-me "election" gave itself away by over-cooking the numbers, the over-indoctrination of students, I mean, attendees by lib-ral NEA (union, no competency testing) teachers and ex-hippie parent/friends cast the die. Absent their depredations, a Trump presidency would not only have been unnecessary; it would not have been possible.

Editrix: Be thankful that it was. Now, thanks to Mr. Trump, the 49% of U. S. who can still think for ourselves has seen our grotesque gov-mint bureaucracy exposed for the slimy swamp that it has become.

THEY SOWED HATRED & DIVISION FOR 4 YEARS, NOW OFFER US UNITY

I didn't say "Democrats", you did. Note: lib-ral "unity": see "obedience".

NEW RULES

Gramma says the teen moron mom is not a slut because both her bastards had the same baby daddy.

NO BELTS, PINS OR PADS

Feminists are all a-tanto. Suck-ups on both sides of the aisle N.O.W. say "women & men". Dilemma: Ain't that like holding a door open for a broad?

HEAVENLY MUSCLE PLUS AMAZING GRACE

When we properly care for our animals then ease their passage, our former charges not only intercede for us, they personally protect us.

A neighbor once sought a confrontation. The poor, dumb bastard. When he faced off with me, he was facing all of us. We must've looked like Goliath.

The poor, dumb bastard.

YOU MIGHT COULD BE A LIB-RAL IF

You are willing to see the blood, sweat and tears of all our patriots go for naught and turn the Country over to a 47-year political hack whose entire family is <u>owned</u> by Communist Fucking China just because your kick-ass President used a politically-incorrect pronoun in a tweet. See also: "progressive".

AMERICAN WOMAN

You elected her husband President of the United States. Twice. You put her on the cover of fashion magazines. You buy her book. Still, she hates your racist guts because you don't recognize her when she walks the dog. Lacking any sense of fairness, you continue to buy mags that mawk Michelle and ignore a true beauty/fashion icon because you dislike her husband. Hear me roar.

ALREADY-WEALTHY WASHINGTON OUTSIDER VS ON-THE-TAKE CAREER BUREAUCRAT

Democrats support a fraudulently elected candidate the claim to respect the wishes of the people. Half of US are OK with this hoax as long as it "keeps our shit coming".

Q: Is Biden the fraud or the hoax?

A: Yes.

NETANYAHU OWES HIM A FAVOR

Trump should enlist the help of Israeli Intelligence in ferreting out the Biden-China connection to the "election" scam. Israel's clandestine services are better than ours and certainly more loyal.

ATT FOX NEWS: DOMINION. Do-min-ion. I'm sure there's a story there somewhere. PS: Trump won. In a landslide.

THE BLUE MARLIN AND THE CARP

One is an exotic beauty with impeccable fashion sense; t'other a so-so who always looks (and usually is) pissed off. Guess which one made all the fashion magazines? What's that? We shouldn't judge a person looks? Tell that to the undoable editor who said, "Melania looks as if she is always about to sneeze", doubtless a reference to her captivating Eurasian eyes. Eat your heart out, fatty.

PS: LGBT-WHATEVER thugs call them both "fish". It is not a compliment.

GEE, THANKS, LIB-RAL MAYORS

Homeowners insurance increases an average of $40-50 a year to cover inflation. This year, expect an additional $400-500 to offset Antifa/BLM thuggery. Ask me how I know.

PS: Lookit your bill. Now you know, too.

Note: No rioting in your town? It don't matter. Insurance works by spreading the risk. People (and mayors) who have their shit together carry those who don't. As usual.

Editrix: So <u>that's</u> why JoeKammy want the red states to bail out the blue ones.

CASUALTIED TO
CRETINISM

Having never heard of Ticonderoga or Dienbienphu, today's Army generals routinely order firebases set up on low ground or, in the case of Outpost Restrepo, at the base of three (3) mountains. Why be near enemy-held high ground when you can be surrounded by it?

Results were predictable to all but our Army brass. No wonder Trump has no patience with these idiots.

GLOBALIST GLOATFEST

######

PICTURE A GLOBAL EARTH DAY. THEY CELE-BRATE: WE THE SHEEPLE CLEAN UP THE MESS.

Well, okay, unlike tree huggers, the globalists won't shit the sidewalk (we think), and they won't toss their granola bar wrappers in the park (we hope).

BI-DE-Numbers

Dispatch: 911. What is your emergency?

Yuppie broad: Alexa! I don't believe in personal protection. Please make this burglar stop beating me until the defunded police arrive. Their response time to my GPS coordinates should be 3-7 minutes if they are not in sensitivity training.

Dispatch: Your call sounds like robber stereotyping. It has been canceled. You may call back when you learn to phrase your request properly, using only approved pronouns*. And stop blowing that fucking whistle!

*You may describe his/her... I mean, its clothing, but not its race, sex, height, and, if it is a female, certainly not her... I mean its weight. Any gender phrasing must be according to LGBT-WTF guidelines. Have a nice day!

NEA VS COVID

Kids at school and online learn nothing. In other words, nothing has changed. Thank a teechr.

YOU BECOME THE INSTRUMENT OF WHAT NEEDS TO BE SAID. -Noel Paul Stookey

Your kid is an honor bumper sticker student at Lake Park elementary school. Pshaw! According to Doc, my 4 year-old Grant is "a poster child for ringworm". Na, na, na na-na. Check out the Terbinafine Calendar, be-yotch. Grant earned himself the pole position in January; little brother Max took the honors in March. Eat your heart out.

PS: Doc has a "diseased" (looks fine to me) heart-in-a-jar in her office, next to her payment plan brochure. Rather than chance it, I paid in full.

CAVE TO COMPUTER

It has happened. Hada by a H-P just to get the news.

Q: Don't you source (yuppie for "get") your news from Fox?

A: 'Till it became the Pablum Angle. Burying the Story of the Century. To find out how Dominion scammed the election one must go online, which is yuppie for "going online". So, I think I'll go to Starbucks?

VOTE HERE

I <u>watched</u> BLM operatives drag in the local drunks and druggies.*All were (too politely) told, "Oh sir, you already mailed in your ballot". There was, of course, no follow-up check of their fraud-by-mail. Gov-mint bureaucrats have no incentive to do anything extra, so they don't.

*Any tenured hoax will tell you, "One person, one vote", and an informed electorate be damned. Ain't democracy wonderful?

BIG GIRL

Yes, Dear, they're lovely. Every man wants to marry a 300 lb. Chick with face, neck and sleeve tattoos plus a piercing at every orifice, but would not that money have been better spent on Jenny Craig? What's that? Try yoga, Pilates and jogging? Nothing worked? Man-up, Missy, and eat a tapeworm. It will "empower" you. Note: At this moment, the guppy draws and man buns are saying, "Eeuuu!". The biker chicks, meanwhile, our thinking, "Ya know, that might could work...".

MAGIC MAN

Tens of people attended his rallies but he gets eighty million votes.

5,000 votes arrive from the military base; only five are for Trump.

Thousands of "extra" New York votes get shipped to Pennsylvania and <u>counted</u>.

"Barack Obama speaks well, and he's clean" gets more black Votes than Obama.

"Integrated schools are interracial jungles" gets more black votes than Obama.

<u>We need this guy</u>. He makes shit happen.

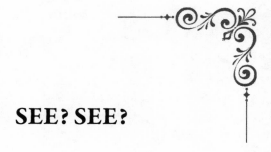

SEE? SEE?

This thing writes itself. "You become... You become
the instrument of what it is that wants to be said."
-Noel Paul Berto

CRAVEN CUOMO COMMUNISM SECTION

#######

F ORMERLY FOX
The story of the century is Smartmatic/Dominion. Let's talk about Joe tripping over his dog.

STATEN ISLAND

NYPD will respond in force if: (pick one)

a) You report looting & burning;

b) You open your business.

Wanna open your bar? Call 911 and say BLM is vandalizing it. NYPD will <u>stay away</u>.

GEORGIA BULLSHIT

Gov, Kemp went on Fox and tried to mealy-mouth his position. It didn't work, <u>and he knew it</u>. Next morning, he announced a recount. Do-dah.

PS: If you are waiting for Laura Ingram to ask His Honor why in the Good Christ (excuse me, Angie) he doesn't order his Attorney General to do his job, and then press Kemp on re-convening the legislature rather than waiting for couple corrupt judges to take their thumbs outta their asses, #MeToo.

Editrix: Heck, I'm still waiting for her to say, "D-D- Dominion". DO-MIN-ION. D-O-M-I-N-I-O-N.

Update! This just in at 2230: "We tried to push Governor Kemp a little bit last night." Yay. Now, that is some hard-hitting reporting, folks.

A DEMOCRAT
OPERATIVE/
POLL WORKER

calls 4 suitcases of ballots "one open bin" with zero explanation of as to why they (it) were (was) hidden under a table, and nobody on The New Fox Network follows up.

GALA WALKIN'
THE DOG
SECTION

#######

I AM FINALLY PROUD OF MY PERMANENT FIRST LADY

"There go the dog walker..."

Michelle is sooo pissed off. First, Trump nixes her husband's "legacy" of taxpayer-funded late-term/partial-birth abortion, pallets of "Please don't hurt U.S." money to Iran, a Paris Accord that makes U.S. pay a zillion bucks to fuck up our own economy while giving heavy polluters like China and India a pass, and the tired trade deals that have put "Made In Communist Fucking China" labels on everything we buy while our own factories crumble into dust. Now Mrs. Obama is in a snit because, "Waa! People don't recognize me when I walk Rover." Translation: "Waa! All the M.V. old money think I'm the help."

Editrix: Aw, the Obiden legacy is secure. They got them Little Sisters of the Poor to lose their white privilege and stop playing the celibacy card as if they are not getting knocked-up in bunches. Even better, they SWAT-raided the Gibson Guitar

Company (you never know when a craftsperson will come at you with an orbital sander) for using the wrong fucking wood. Now, <u>that</u> is a legacy that lasts.

~~SOURCES~~ RELIABLE SOURCES SAY

"So, aren't ballots <u>always</u> kept in suitcases?"

Q: If an anonymous anti-Trumpet whistleblower is a hero to CNN, what is a poll worker who stands up in court under oath?

A: Ignored.

THE ANTI-ESTABLISHMENT ESTABLISHMENT

Then: The left is anti-war, anti-big gov-mint, anti-big banks.

Now: The left picks a 47-year political hack over a populist DC outsider who is anti-war, anti-big gov-mint, anti-big banks.

Q: Is this irony?

A: Stupidity.

Q: Don't that make them the useful idiots of Marx & Engels?

A: Don'tcarehatetrump.

Att lib-rals: If you think cherry-picking whistleblowers to bolster your bias is cool, you're <u>really</u> gonna like:

WEIRD SCIENCE ACCORDING TO CNN

1-A corporate conglomerate outlet packed with people cannot covid spread.

2-a mom & pop restaurant at 25% capacity will fucking kill you.

Q: Gee, d'ya think Obiden's buddies in Big Tech/Media/
Banks are corporatists?

A: Don'tcarehatetrump.

Q: WHAT HAPPENS WHEN a liberal is forced to stand up
and say, "Black Lives Matter"?

A: A conservative.

INTEGRITY VS DEMAGOGUERY

You are a computer-savvy lifetime lib-ral. You look at the
stats of the Biden/China/Dominion "election" hoax and say,
"No Fucking Way", and... and you share your o-o-opinion with
your lib-ral friends.

Q: What happens when you get doxxed, listed and
shunned?

A: Another conservative.

MOVE OVER, MAO

Just for Joe, Democrat machine operatives have conjured the "Office of the President-Elect", which is apparently Play Skool for fraudulently-elected... frauds. Hopefully, that will be the extent of our China Connection's "Legacy" and we will get to keep our Country.

Also by Phil Berto:
SNIPPETS – COMMENTS FROM THE RED
SNIPPED – AMERICA POST #ME TOO
SNIPS – COMMENTS FROM THE BLACK AND BLUE
SNAPPED – COMMENTS FROM A C-C-CONSERVA-
TIVE
SNAPPER – THE LIBERAL FINGER
UNSNAPPED – OBEDIENT LIB-RAL EDITION
FIVE SLEAZY SLIPPETS AND A MISSIVE OR TWO
VISIT WWW.PHILBERTO.COM[1]

---

1. http://WWW.PHILBERTO.COM/

Made in the USA
Columbia, SC
10 March 2021